Made in United States
Troutdale, OR
12/15/2023

15890580R00056